Network Marketing as a Career

How to Earn a Full-Time Income in Your Part-Time Business

David M. Ward

Network Marketing as a Career
(c) David M. Ward. All rights reserved.

http://goldenlanternbooks.com

Free Recruiting Tips Newsletter

Get more recruiting tips with my **FREE Recruiting Tips Newsletter**. You'll also be notified when I release new books or have a special offer.

To subscribe, go to: http://recruitandgrowrich.com/newsletter

Contents

Can you really earn a full-time income in a part-time business?

Can you really earn a full-time income in a part-time networking marking business? Absolutely. I've done it and so have countless others. In this book, you'll learn how you can do it, too.

You don't need a business background or any network marketing experience. You don't need a lot of time or money. You don't need to know a lot of people. If you have a strong desire to improve your life, if you're coachable and willing to work, you can build a successful network marketing business.

Millions of people earn extra income in a part-time network marketing business. Hundreds of thousands earn $50,000 to $100,000 a year. My company alone has hundreds of six- and seven-figure income earners and many thousands of distributors earning thousands of dollars per month.

If they can do it, you can do it.

In fact, this is one of the key features of the network marketing business model. It's something anybody can do. Think about it, if you had to have exceptional talent to make money in network marketing there would be relatively few successful distributors, not millions.

I'm not saying everyone earns good money. Not at all. If you don't do the work (or give it enough time), you're not going to make much money.

Yes, it takes work. Yes, it takes time. It's a business. And like any business, if you want to succeed, you have to put in the time and effort.

Want some good news? It's a lot easier to build a network marketing business than most "regular" businesses.

You don't need thousands of dollars or tens of thousands of dollars to get started. You don't have to pay rent, hire employees, or spend a fortune on advertising. Your company takes care of the products or services, shipping, accounting, and customer service. They create the websites, apps, videos, and brochures. They do all of that, and more, so you can focus on the one thing they don't do—marketing.

And yet, you can earn as much in a network marketing business as you can in any small business.

But that's not why I started a network marketing business. I started because I wanted to earn *passive* income, something most traditional businesses don't offer.

For most of my career, I was an attorney in private practice. I made a great income, but I was always working. After twenty ears, the long hours and constant stress were catching up with me.

I needed a Plan B.

I wanted something I could do part-time that could provide a full-time income and enough passive income so I could eventually retire.

I'd tried network marketing before but didn't stick with it. I told myself it wasn't for me and I'd have to find another way to build passive income. I started a traditional business (publishing) but found myself working more hours, not less.

One day, an attorney friend asked for my opinion about a network marketing company he'd heard about. I took a look and liked what I saw. I liked it a lot.

I'd told myself network marketing wasn't for me, but this company was different. This was something I could see myself doing. After some research, I signed up as a distributor.

I started out a few hours a week. In less than six months, I was earning several thousand dollars per month, still working part time. I kept going and within a few years I was earning a six-figure passive income that allowed me to retire from the practice of law.

Today, I spend most of my time doing things I enjoy, things I never had time to do before.

There's a lesson in this. The lesson is that while you can make money with just about any network marketing company, if you want to have long-term success, you should align yourself with a company that offers products or services or a cause you believe in and want to share with the world.

I didn't do that in the past. Like many distributors, I signed up with the first company I saw.

Don't do that. Don't sign up just for the money. Find a company that's right for you.

Check out the company. Try the products or services. Talk to some distributors and customers, attend some events, and ask lots of questions. See what you can learn and what your gut tells you.

And then, when you sign up, treat your business like a real business.

Many distributors don't. They treat it like a hobby. They work the business when they find some extra time. That's not a formula for success.

To succeed in network marketing, you must make your business a priority in your life. Among other things, that means that when you're working, even if it's just one hour a day, you focus 100% on the business.

I have a friend who calls this having "a career mindset". When you have it, you'll be able to join a long list of distributors who earn a full-time income in their part-time business.

If you're thinking about starting a business (or have recently started one), this book will show what it takes to build a successful network marketing business. You'll learn how to get the business off to a good start and quickly earn some income.

If you've been in network marketing for a while and your business isn't growing as quickly as you would like, this book will show you how to get back on track. You'll learn how to grow your team, increase your income, and achieve your goals.

If you're an experienced network marketer who wants to build your income to six-figures and beyond, this book shows you how I did it and how you can, too.

You'll learn

- How to earn your first $1,000 (and why you need to do it FAST)
- How I got to $4,000 per month in less than six-months
- How to recruit more distributors and BETTER distributors
- How to overcome fear and procrastination
- How to schedule your day, week and month and how to stay on schedule
- Why some distributors grow faster than others—and how to speed up your journey
- Why you're only one recruit away from explosive growth
- Why it's EASIER to build your business quickly rather than slowly

- How to develop as a leader (and develop other leaders) and multiply your growth
- The BEST advice my upline ever game me
- And more!

You'll learn how to get to $1,000 per month, $4,000 per month, and $10,000 per month, and what to expect along the way. You'll see my actual numbers—how much I earned my first month, my first six months, my first year, and each year thereafter, on my way to a six-figure income.

Here's how this material is organized:

Chapter 1: Earning your first $1,000

The most important part of any new business is getting it started. It's also the most difficult. This chapter shows you what to do to earn your "belief check" and why it is vital that you do.

Chapter 2: Getting to $1,000 per month

When you are earning $1,000 per month, you have a real business. To accomplish this, you need to learn a simple system for contacting prospects and showing them your products or services and business opportunity. This chapter shows you what that system looks like and how to create a "daily method of operation" so you can accomplish this as soon as possible.

Chapter 3: Getting to $4,000 per month

Earning a consistent $4,000 per month is a turning point for many distributors. It is often the point where they give up their job or other business and put more time into building their network marketing career. This chapter shows you how to work with your customers and your team to scale up your business with less effort.

Chapter 4: Getting to $10,000 per month (and beyond)

This chapter shows you why you're closer to $10,000 a month than you realize and how to develop the leadership skills that will help you take your business to the next level.

Chapter 5: What it REALLY takes to reach the top

If your sponsor is like my sponsor, they didn't tell you certain things about network marketing you need to know. In this chapter, you'll learn the truth about network marketing that will allow you to get to build a successful career.

Yes, you can earn a full-time income in your part-time network marketing business. Turn the page and I'll show you what to do.

Chapter 1: Earning Your First $1,000

Some people say that your first check in network marketing is your "belief check". Before you get that first check or direct deposit, you don't know if the business works or if you can be successful in it. Your doubts and fears can defeat you before you've had a chance to find out.

As a new distributor, your most important task is to get paid as quickly as possible.

Once you get paid, things change. You know the business works. Your belief level and confidence goes way up. If someone says, "nobody makes money in network marketing," or tells you to "start a *real* business" or "get a job," you know better. You've already made money in your business.

When you earn your first $1,000, there's no turning back. You've covered your startup costs and earned a nice profit. You know what to say to prospects, what to give them, and how to sign them up and help them get their business started.

That's the essence of network marketing. You learn what to do, you do it, and you teach it to others who repeat the process.

You also have a great story to tell your prospects. Your story can make you a lot of money.

When you show someone your business and they ask you how you're doing, you'll be able to tell them you've already earned

$1,000, got a raise and a promotion and you're on your way to your next one, and. . . you're just getting started.

What do you think will happen? They'll want to know how you did it. And how they can do it, too.

Earning your first $1,000 is everything. Let's talk about how to do it.

MAKE YOUR GOAL VISIBLE

As soon as you can, talk to your sponsor or upline leader and ask them what you need to do to earn your first $1,000.

Can you do it with personal sales? How many? Which products?

How many distributors do you need to sign up and how much do they need to buy or sell (to distributors or customer)?

Are there any time limits? Are there any qualifying or "fast start" bonuses when you get promoted? Can you earn any bonuses for helping your distributors get promoted? How much time do you have to do this?

Have them go over the comp plan with you and show you how much you earn at each level for each sale you make, and how much you earn in overrides when someone on your team makes a sale. Have them show you how to get your first promotion.

Ask them to give you a few examples of what other distributors have done to earn their first $1,000. Write these down and post them where you will see them every day.

When I was got started, I drew out the proverbial network marketing "circles" you often see at presentations. I put my name at the top of the page, circled it, and drew additional circles beneath my name, representing distributors I needed to recruit and "legs" I needed to build. At first, those circles were blank and I knew that to get promoted I needed to fill them in.

This allowed me to see what I needed to do. Making it visible made it possible. All I needed to do was fill in those circles.

As I recruited distributors, I added their names to my chart. When someone on my team recruited someone, I added their name, too.

Making it visible helped me to get my business off to a good start. I suggest you do the same. Map it out for you so you'll know what you have to do to earn your "belief check".

Now, it may turn out that for your company's comp plan and your work schedule, earning $1,000 quickly may not be realistic. That's okay. Earning your first $500 or getting your first promotion, your first override or your first bonus can also qualify as your belief check.

The point is to choose a short-term goal that gets you excited when you imagine yourself achieving it and that will make a good story to share with prospects.

GETTING STARTED RIGHT

Now that you have a goal and a visual representation of what you need to do, it's time to launch your business. Here's what I suggest you do:

If you haven't done so, use your product or service. This will help build your belief in your company and its products and give you another story to share with prospects who will want to know how the product has worked for you. Also talk to other distributors and/or customers about how they have benefited from the product or service. Learn their stories so you can share them with others.

You should also collect distributor stories. Talk to your upline leaders and others in the company and find out (a) their background, (b) why they got started in the business, and (c) what they've accomplished and/or are working to accomplish.

When I got started, I told all of my prospects my upline's story. If the prospect was an attorney (I recruited a lot of my colleagues), I told them about other attorneys who were distributors and how they were doing in the business. I also told them why I got started and what I wanted to accomplish. Later, when I had some success, I shared my results.

If you're like me (and you are!), these stories will not only motivate you, they will help you recruit other distributors.

Start writing your story. Write down why you got started and what you want to accomplish. What does the business mean to you?

Order inventory. You'll need something to show (and sell) to prospects. If your company offers samples you can give to prospects, make sure you get a supply of these, too.

Set up your distributor website so you have a place to send prospects and sign them up. Order tools (DVDs, brochures, etc.) to hand out.

Register for the training class(es) (local or online) offered by your company and/or upline organization. Make sure you attend. Promise yourself you'll bring one or more distributors with you to the next class as soon as you recruit them.

Attend a live business presentation in your area. Introduce yourself to the speaker, host, and other leaders. Sit in the front row and take notes. Pay attention to the stories told by the speaker and the testimonials at the end of the presentation. Events like these will help you build your business. Commit to coming to the next presentation or meeting and bringing one or more prospects with you.

Set up a time to meet with your sponsor or upline leader to do a "game plan," to establish goals and a plan of action for getting your business started.

Finally, start your list of contacts.

MAKE YOUR LIST

One of the first (and most important) steps in starting your network marketing business is to make a list of prospects. People you know are your "warm market" and you should contact them first to show them your products and business opportunity.

Some network marketing trainers say you shouldn't approach your warm market first. They say you should wait until you have some experience and some success before you contact your warm market because people who know you may be harder to "impress." They are also more likely to tell you all about how network marketing doesn't work and discourage you.

These trainers say you should start in the "cold market," meaning people you don't know. Because they don't know you, they won't know you're new and you won't care what they say or think because unlike your warm market you'll never have to speak to them again. There is some truth to this. It is easier to ignore a stranger who turns you down than someone you care about and will see again and again.

The cold market is also unlimited. You may know a few hundred people but there are hundreds of thousands of prospects available to you in the cold market.

Still, I recommend you start with your warm market. Here's why:

- You already have a list and contact them immediately. You don't have to spend money to buy leads or advertise, or spend time networking to find prospects.

- You can talk to the people on your list. Your warm market knows and trusts you. When you contact them, they'll talk to you. If they miss your call, they'll call you back. Cold market prospects may screen calls, ignore messages, and hang up on people they don't know.
- You can ask your warm market for a favor—to look at some information or watch a video, for example, and give you their opinion. This is an effective, no-pressure way to show people what you offer. That's not as easy to do in the cold market.
- You can also ask your warm market for referrals to prospects who might be interested in your products or in earning extra income. This is also not as easy to do in the cold market.
- When a prospect in your warm market asks a question, you can tell them you are new and don't know the answer and then get help from your sponsor or another distributor. In the cold market, that's not only awkward, it makes prospects question why they should even talk to you.
- If your prospects sign up in the business, you get to work with people you care about. If you wait to approach them until after you're successful, they may resent you for not telling them about the business from the beginning.
- If you wait and they sign up with another distributor and build a big business under them, you will kick yourself!

Network marketing is primarily a warm market business. It's about contacting people you know and when they sign up, helping them contact people they know. You can't do that effectively if you haven't approached your own warm market.

The cold market has advantages, but it is more difficult to approach. Start with your warm market, learn the business with a comparatively "easy" crowd, and then, when you know what you're doing, you can approach the cold market.

Make your list and include everyone you know. Don't prejudge anyone. You never know who will or won't be interested or who will or won't be good at the business. Trust me, you will be wrong almost as often as you are right. I've seen more than a few distributors misjudge people and not approach them, only to see them at an event as someone else's guest or a new distributor on someone else's team.

Besides, if someone isn't interested, they can give you referrals. And if they're interested in the business, they might become a customer.

Many people on your list won't be interested in anything. That's okay. That's normal. Stay in touch with them. As their circumstances change, they may suddenly be interested.

I've signed up distributors five and even 10 years after I first spoke to them about the business. This would never have happened if I hadn't put them on my list.

CONTACT YOUR LIST

During your game plan (or at another time) your sponsor or upline trainer will go over your list with you to help you determine who to contact first and the best way to approach them.

They might suggest you start with the "easy" people on your list. These are folks who are likely to buy your product or service simply because they like you and want to help you start your business. They're at least willing to look at what you are offering. Starting with "easy" people on your list should allow you to get some sales and distributors.

Your trainer may also help you identify your "best" prospects. These are people who have business experience, especially with network marketing, professionals, people who know a lot of people, and people who are highly motivated to earn more income or start a new career.

Your sponsor or trainer should then coach you on how to approach your prospects. They should show you different approaches, tell you what to say and do, and recommend the tools that might be best suited to your prospects. They may also help you speak to your prospects.

We'll talk about approaches in the next chapter.

USE THE PHONE

Network marketing is a people business. You have to meet with prospects or talk to them on the phone. Unfortunately, many distributors try to build their business by doing everything online.

You can use email, text, social media, and messaging to set up a time to talk, confirm an appointment, and deliver information, but it is not a substitute for speaking with prospects.

You need to talk to prospects to make sure you have their attention. They need to hear the excitement and urgency in your voice. You need to hear how they respond, ask questions and listen to their questions, and determine whether they are also excited about what you're showing them or just being polite.

If you're going to show them how your business can help them get what they want, you need to know what that is. You need to talk to your prospects about what they want and why they want it.

You also need to speak to them to get them to commit to meeting you, coming to your event, watching your video or dialing into your call. You need to speak to them to confirm the date and time they will visit your website or review your materials so you can schedule a date and time to follow-up.

You can't do this effectively without talking to them.

Many distributors don't use the phone because they're looking for a shortcut, an "easy" way to connect with many prospects. They may be nervous and want to hide behind technology.

Trust me. I've tried everything and without a doubt, a phone call is the best way to contact a prospect. It's the best way to get their attention and the best way to get them to look at some information, and if they don't look at the information, they are a guaranteed "no".

That's true in both the warm and cold markets. And in the cold market, where other distributors are trying to connect with them on social media and email and text, when you call them on the phone, you will truly stand out.

Top recruiters, top money-earners, build their business on the phone.

Your sponsor or trainer should listen to you speak to some prospects and coach you on ways to improve what you say and what you do. They may ask you to introduce your prospects to them over the phone and let *them* present the information or invite the prospect to the event, while you listen, learn and earn.

On the other hand, they may not offer to do this, or you may not want them to. Some distributors are more comfortable doing it on their own. At least have your sponsor or trainer do some role playing with you before you begin. They should also make themselves available via a 3-way call, to answer your prospect's questions and invite them to take the next step.

When you talk to your prospects, use your newness to your advantage. Your warm market (probably) knows you're just getting started in the business; don't pretend otherwise. In fact, if they don't know you're just getting started, tell them this. That way, when they have questions, you can say, "I don't know". This gives you the perfect excuse to get your sponsor on the phone to speak with them, which is what you want.

Telling prospects you are new will no doubt allow you to be more relaxed. You're just sharing information with a friend, with no pressure on them to buy anything. When you relax, they'll be more likely to relax and just look at the information without feeling pressure to buy anything or do anything.

Also, tell your prospects your story—why you're doing this, what you want to accomplish and why it's important to you. Are you determined to increase your income so that your spouse can quit their job or so you can pay off some debts or so you can build retirement income? Tell your prospects your "why". It might make them more willing to help you and, if they want what you want, they may be more inclined to sign up as a distributor.

Also share your upline's story. That's what I did when I was getting started. I told prospects my upline's story—his background, why he joined the business, and what he had accomplished so far. I told my prospects I wanted to do what he had done and explained that he was helping me to do it. Many of my prospects wanted the same things I wanted (time freedom, retirement income) and signed up.

Learn your upline's story. As you meet more distributors, learn their stories, too, especially people with different backgrounds. When you talk to a prospect who is a school teacher, for example, you'll be able to tell them about the distributor you know who is also a teacher.

You should also be prepared to tell "product stories"—benefits you've received from the product or service or benefits received by others. Not everyone wants to start a business (or is ready to) but they may be open to trying your products or giving you referrals to people they know who also want those benefits.

Why so much emphasis on stories? Why not just share the facts? Because stories have people in them and people are more interesting than facts. We watch movies because we relate to the people and get involved in their stories. We want to know what happens to them—do they get the girl, win the prize, or defeat the enemy?

The facts are important, too. But people buy for emotional reasons. They buy your products or sign up in your business to get the benefits they offer. They use the facts to justify their decision, so don't ignore them, but don't expect them to buy just because of them.

Nobody will sign up in your business because your company has a patent or is about to open in another country. Those are factual, but by themselves, not persuasive. People sign up in the business because they want to change their life and enjoy the freedom of being in their own business. They want to work from home so they can spend more time with their family. They want to pay off their credit card debt or send their kids to college.

That's why they sign up in your business.

Learn the facts and learn the stories. Facts tell but stories sell.

EARN YOUR FIRST $1,000

They have a name for it. It's called the "can't sleep phase". It's when you start your network marketing business and you're so excited you have trouble sleeping.

You keep paper next to your bed so you can add names to your list. You think about the business all day long. You don't know much yet—all you know is that you've (finally) found the way to accomplish your goals and take your life in a new direction and you are *excited*.

That can't sleep phase is golden. It feels great, and it's the key to getting your business off to a great start. That's because your prospects will see your excitement and want to know what's going on in your life.

They'll want to hear your story. They'll want to watch your video, come to your meet, or visit your website, to see "what it's all about."

You don't need to know all the information. You just need to get busy and contact everyone you know.

That's how I earned my first $1,000. That's how you will earn yours.

You may not have a big warm market. That's okay. Since you're just getting started and haven't talked to anybody, your list is virgin territory. Since nobody has seen your products or business, you are much more likely to get some yeses.

Some prospects will buy something to help you out. Some will sign up as a distributor for the same reason. And some will see what you see about the business opportunity and get excited about doing what you're doing.

Even better, most of the people who sign up as distributors will also have a list of prospects that is a clean slate. That means they can also quickly get some results. As they get sales and recruits and get promoted, you'll get promoted, too.

Okay, you're excited and you have a list of people to contact. You've learned (or will learn) some basics at your game plan and training. You have inventory and/or tools and you're ready to show people what you offer.

What's next?

You talk to everyone you can as quickly as you can. Speed is important. Don't think about what you're doing or what someone may say. Don't think about results, just take action.

If someone isn't interested, move on to the next person on your list. You might come back to them later, to see if things have changed, but you might be so busy working with the ones who sign up it's not a priority.

THE 90-DAY RUN

Network marketing distributors often talk about "going on a 90-day run". That means for a 90-day period, they put as much time and energy into the business as they can. They run so they can make things happen.

This is what I did to get my business started.

I could only put a few hours a week into the business but I made good use of that time.

I suggest you do the same.

Run, as fast as you can. Don't walk, don't take your time, don't try to do everything perfectly. Take massive income. Talk everyone you can as quickly as you can.

This is not the time to organize your notes or design fancy labels for your tools. This is the time for action.

Your attitude should be, "Everyone needs to see this; my job is to show it to them. If they like it, great. If they don't, no problem. I'm not going to pressure them or try to convince them they should be interested. That's not my job. I have other people to talk to."

And call the next person on your list.

Focus on the process, not the outcome. Focus on contacting prospects and inviting them to look at some information. Focus on that, not whether they buy or sign up as a distributor.

Invite enough prospects to see some information and you will get some results.

Right now, you don't need to know much about the products; your enthusiasm for the ones you use or the ones you've seen others use is more than enough.

You don't need to understand the entire comp plan. Learn a story or two about some people who are making money and use those.

You don't need to be able to answer questions. You have a support team who can do that for you.

You don't need to be good. You just need to be busy. Contact enough prospects and everything will sort itself out.

If there are 100 people on your list, contact all of them in your first few days. Most will say no. That's okay. Some will look at some information and some will buy something and/or sign up in the business.

Once you get your first sale and/or distributor, your confidence will soar, Keep running and soon you'll get your next one. Before you know it, you'll get your first promotion, your first bonus, and you'll be on your way to earning your first $1,000.

I don't know how long it will take you. All I know is that if you have the desire to succeed and you make enough calls and trust the process, it will happen. I also know that when it does happen, you'll be even more excited and ready to get to the next level.

Every company is different, with different products and price points, commissions and bonuses, so my results won't tell you much about what's possible for you. In fact, my results might discourage you. Not because I did well but because I didn't. You see, in my first month I only earned $200. Not much, but enough for me to see I could do it. It allowed me to relax and do what I've told you to do—talk to everyone and trust the process.

That's what I did and in my second month I earned $600. I was moving in the right direction.

In my third month, I earned $1,800. Now we're talking. I had crossed the $1,000 threshold and was on my way to bigger and better things. The following month—my fourth—I earned $2300. In my fifth month, I earned $3,500, and I never looked back.

It didn't happen because I was good. It happened because I had a burning desire to make something happen and I took massive action.

You can do it, too.

Think less, do more. Talk to everyone. Find out if they want to (or are willing to) look at some information about what you're doing.

Move quickly and get this done. When the dust settles and you've achieved your goal, you can organize your notes and take a day off.

And then get ready to get to the next level, $1,000 per month.

Chapter 2: Getting to $1,000 per month

If you can earn $1,000, you can earn $1,000 a month. At first, you'll probably do that primarily through personal production, through commissions earned on products purchased by the distributors you sign up and by customers who aren't interested in the business. As customers renew or reorder products, you'll earn additional commissions. You may earn bonuses, too.

Eventually, you'll earn overrides on the production of your team. When they sign up a customer or a distributor who places an order, you'll get overrides on that production. (Note: check your comp plan to see what you need to do to qualify for overrides.)

Overrides are passive income. Someone else does the work, and you get paid. When I earned $1,000 per month in my business, I was excited. But nothing compares to how I felt when I began earning $1,000 per month in overrides.

Earning $1,000 per month of passive income is a significant achievement. To earn that much with a bank account, you would need to deposit $328,500 and earn 3.88% interest.

Not bad, is it?

How do you get there? By learning a simple recruiting system, following that system, and teaching that system to the distributors on your team. When you do that, and they do the same thing, your team will eventually produce enough sales to provide you with $1,000 per month in overrides.

What is the system? It's a way of conducting the business that every distributor can do.

Not every distributor can deliver a good presentation, for example, (or wants to do that), so trying to teach everyone how to do a presentation would not be an effective system. Everyone can give prospects their website and ask them to watch a video, however. Everyone can invite prospects to dial into a conference call or come to an event.

When you follow a system that everyone can follow, duplication can take place. When that happens, your team and income grow without your active participation. That's why it's called passive income.

At your game plan, or in the company or team training, you should have learned about the system your upline organization uses. You should have learned that it's best to use tools (websites, brochures, videos, etc.) or other distributors (e.g., at a business presentation, sit-down, conference call, etc.) instead of doing the presentation yourself.

Don't explain anything. Don't do the presentation yourself. Use the tools and other distributors to do that for you. That's something anyone can do.

Note, if you can do the presentation, and you want to, it's okay to do it for other distributor's prospects, just not your own. For example, you might do it at your local event or on a recruiting call conducted by your upline organization. Prospects can see that the distributor who invited them to see or hear the presentation isn't doing the presentation, someone else is (you).

How is this different?

If a prospect sees the distributor who invited them to the presentation doing that presentation, the prospect will think that if they sign up, they will have to do the presentation for his or her prospects. Many prospects don't want to do that or think they can do that. They may not sign up as a distributor for that reason alone.

Show prospects that your business is something they can do and you'll have more prospects joining your business.

For the same reason, you should be careful about answering your prospect's questions. It's better to introduce them to another distributor (e.g., your upline) and let them answer the questions.

Using tools and events and other distributors to present the information and answer questions is an effective system because everyone can do these things, and they can do them immediately after they get started. That allows your team to grow quickly.

Prospects see you didn't do the presentation, you sent them to your website. They see that when they asked questions, you introduced them to another distributor to answer them. Prospects think, "I can do that," and they can.

Prospects judge your business opportunity based on what they see you do. If you show them a complicated, time-consuming system that makes them think they have to learn and do a lot of complicated things, few prospects will sign up.

Show them a business that's simple and doesn't take a lot of time (e.g., handing out videos, sending people to a website, inviting people to an event), and more prospects will sign up. And when they sign up, they'll know what to do.

That's when duplication takes place.

Your team will do what you do, not what you say. Follow the system and they will, too.

THE EXPOSURE PROCESS

Your job is to approach prospects, show them information about your products and business, and find out if they are interested in learning more. When you do that, you're doing an "exposure".

What's the best way to approach a prospect? What do you say and do?

There are two basic approaches. They're easy to use (so everyone can use them) and they both work.

The *Direct Approach* is about as simple as it gets. You tell the prospect you want to show them something that might interest them and then you show it to them. You can invite them to come to a presentation or sit down with them and watch a video together. Or you can give them a tool or website to look at on their own.

You might tell them why you started the business and why you thought they might be interested in doing what you're doing.

The other approach is the *Indirect Approach.* Here, you ask the prospect for a favor.

You tell them what you're doing and ask them to look at some information about what you're doing and give you their opinion. Or, you might ask them to look at some information and let you know if they know anyone who might be interested in looking at some information, in other words, a referral.

The advantage to the indirect approach is that it takes the pressure off the prospect. You're not asking them to buy anything or sign up for anything, you're just asking them for feedback (opinion) or a referral.

You might say, "I'm working on a business project/I've started a new business, and I'd love to get your feedback. Could you take a look at some information and let me know what you think? I'd really appreciate it."

You show them the same information no matter which approach you use. The approach is merely how you get their attention.

SHOW, DON'T TELL

When I got started in the business, they taught me not to explain anything to prospects. They told me there were three reasons:

1) It saves time.

You don't have to learn the presentation or spend 45 minutes delivering it to each prospect. Hand them a tool, invite them to the event, give them the link, and move onto your next prospect.

2) The tool does a better job.

Prospects get to see and hear the information in pure form, unfiltered by your interpretation or presentation, or by their impression of you.

If you don't have any business experience, for example, prospects may not take you seriously. When they see a corporate produced video or come to a live business presentation, however, they get to see top presenters deliver the information. They also get to hear testimonials and success stories.

It's not YOU telling your cousin how you will make a lot of money with this business, it's top money-earners telling them how they've already earned a lot of money, changed their life, and so on. Much more compelling.

3) It duplicates.

"Don't do what works, do what duplicates," they told me.

You want your prospects to see that they don't need to learn a presentation or take the time to deliver it. They don't need to be able to answer a lot of questions. When they see that "all you did" was hand them a tool or give them a website or sit down and show them some information, they see something they can do.

FOLLOW UP

Most people don't sign up or buy something the first time they see it. Some do but you should assume that you will have to follow-up with most of your prospects, often many times.

If you're not showing them the information on the spot, that is, if you're sending them to your website or giving them something to take home and look at on their own, you need to find out *when* they intend to look at the information and *schedule* a time to follow-up.

Ask them when they will watch the video, for example. What day and time? Then, let them know you'll call them to get their feedback. Schedule that day and time in your calendar and let them know you'll be calling on the day and time. This is makes it more likely that they will watch or look at the information and be ready when you call.

A "NO" IS AS GOOD AS A YES

Successful distributors know a "no" is as good as a yes. When you get a no, the prospect is doing you a favor. You no longer have to talk to them or following up with them; you can eliminate them (at least for now) and spend your time talking to other prospects.

Successful distributors focus on the activity—contacting prospects and offering to show them information—not on the result.

When a prospect tells them they're not interested, they think, "Some will, some won't, so what, someone else is waiting, NEXT!" I say (to myself) something similar: "Tell me yes or tell me no but tell me quick, I've got to go!"

If a prospect isn't interested, we thank them and move on. We don't try to convince them they *should* be interested. We don't want to push them or annoy them. If they say no, move on.

We're not in sales. We're in network marketing. We don't try to persuade people.

First, it doesn't work. If you have to persuade people to sign up as a distributor, you will have to persuade them to work the business. Ugh. You want people to sign up because they *want* to, because they're excited and eager to go to work, not because you talked them into it.
Second, it won't duplicate. Most people don't want to sell. If your prospects think they must do what you did, i.e., talk people into signing up or buying, they won't want to become a distributor.

If a prospect isn't interested, move along. A no is as good as a yes.

But this doesn't mean we never follow-up with them. We do, to see if things have changed for them.

Someone who isn't interested today could be very much interested at a later date. Times change, people change, circumstances change. An illness, loss of a job, the birth of a baby, high debts, and other life changes often help prospects reconsider what they previously said didn't interest them. I've signed up many distributors who weren't interested the first time I spoke to them and you will, too.

Assume that a "no" means "not now" and stay in touch with your prospects. But don't push them. Don't try to convince them to change their mind.

Go through your list, contact everyone, and ask them to look at some information. When they agree to look, give them the information and schedule a follow-up. If they say no, thank them and contact the next person on your list.

When you follow-up with someone who has agreed to look at the information, see if they're ready to take the next step. What's the next step? To buy something, sign up as a distributor. If they're not ready to do that, invite them to see more information—come to a live event, look at your website, dial into your conference call.

Our job is to move prospects from exposure to exposure. When they're ready to sign up, you sign them up.

If a prospect has questions, great. That usually means they're interested. Introduce them to your sponsor or another distributor to answer their questions and invite them to sign up.

If they buy something, great. If they sign up as a distributor, great. Help them get their business started and duplicate what you did.

If this sounds simple, it is. It has to be, so everyone can do it.

MONEY LOVES SPEED

If you want to build a big income in network marketing, you have to contact a lot of prospects. Remember, most people say no.

If you do only two or three exposures a day, it might be a long time between sign-ups, which can become discouraging and make it difficult to build momentum. Top money-earners make five, ten, twenty calls a day. Some do many more. That's why they sign up more distributors.

You may not be able to (or want to) do this when you're getting started but you should make as many calls as possible. The more prospects you talk to, the more you will sign up. It really is a numbers game.

To maximize the number of prospects they speak to each day, successful network marketers "compress time". They keep their prospect list in front of them so they can move quickly through the list. As soon as they end one call, they dial the next number.

They spend little time talking to each prospect. Remember, they're not trying to convince anyone to do anything, they just want to find out if they will. Yes or no. They will either look or they won't. If they won't look, top recruiters thank them and move on. If they agree to look, they schedule the date and time to follow-up.

They move quickly through their list, eliminating the ones who aren't interested so they can spend their time talking to the ones who are. This is called "sorting".

Building a business quickly is easier than doing it slowly. Slow is painful. There's too much time between positive outcomes. Building quickly is easier because your next "yes" is right around the corner.

Look at it this way. Let's say you do 30 exposures and get three prospects to say yes and sign up. 27 say no. Ten percent is good but if you do those exposures over a period of two months, each "no" is hard on you and you can get discouraged, especially if it is the first 27 who say no. If you do those 30 exposures in a day or two, however, the "noes" don't bother you because you have three who said yes and can sign them up and work with them.

The ones who make it to the top in network marketing sort and build their business quickly.

ESTABLISH YOUR 'DAILY METHOD OF OPERATION'

It's time to get organized and disciplined about how you spend your time.

First up, start with the big picture. Establish some goals.

Start with your vision of where you want to be five years from now. If you have a magic wand and could create your ideal future what would it look like? What you be doing? How much would you be earning? What kind of work would you be doing?

Write this down in a few paragraphs. Look at it often. Modify it as you make progress.

Next, write down your one-year goal. Where do you want to be twelve months from today? This should be consistent with your five-year vision.

Your one-year goal should include a monetary element but it could also include other things: the number of distributors on your team, your rank in the business, monthly production (individual and/or team), and so on.

Don't spend a lot of time on this right now, or get too detailed. This is just a basic view of the direction you'd like to take your business.

When I was getting started, my goal was to be earning $10,000 per month by my twelfth month. The goal was a stretch because I'd never built a network marketing business, but I knew it was possible because I'd met distributors who had done this and more. If they could do it, I could do it.

I didn't hit that goal but I know I earned more than I would have if I hadn't set this goal.

Once you have established your one-year goal, next up is create a monthly plan to reach that goal.

Get out your calendar and schedule the following:

1) Monthly planning session

Schedule a 30-minute appointment with yourself at the beginning of each month to review your progress and plan the month ahead.

During your monthly planning sessions, add all the upcoming events for the month to your calendar—business presentations, trainings, in-home events, team calls, recruiting calls, webinars, etc. Also add monthly, quarterly, and annual team and corporate events.

Then, write down the activities you plan to do in the coming month.

- How many prospects do you plan to contact each workday?
- How many events will you attend each week? Which ones?
- How many guests do you intend to invite to those events?
- How many new contacts (leads, prospects) will you add to your prospect list each week?

And so on.

If you don't know the answer, just pick a number. See how things go and adjust that number, up or down, for the next month.

Note that planning means focusing on what you will do, not the outcomes of those activities. You can control your activities, not your results. Make sure you plan activities you know you can do or that are a bit of a stretch. Don't choose a number that's completely out of reach.

Also write down "results" goals for the month, in the following categories:

- Number of distributors you will recruit
- Sales volume
- Level/rank you will achieve by the end of the month
- How much you want to earn for the month

As you build a team, also record their monthly goals because what they do will affect your results.

2) Weekly review

Once a week, perhaps on Sunday morning or evening, examine your activities for the previous week and the results you achieved.

How many events did you attend? How many guests did you invite? How many showed up? How many recruits did you sign up? How many sales?

What goals did you achieve or are you on track for? What do you need to adjust?

Ask yourself, "What did I do well?" and "What can I do better?"

Write down your answers and what you will do differently in the coming week.

3) Daily activity

A daily method of operation is a checklist of things you do each day to advance your business. Your checklist should include things like:

- Contacting new prospects/exposures
- Following-up with prospects you've already contacted/exposed
- Inviting prospects upcoming events
- Game plans with new distributors
- Check-ins with your team
- Listening to team calls

The best way to make sure you get your work done is to schedule it. Add to your calendar each work day one or more blocks of time dedicated to doing your work.

You might schedule a block of two hours in the morning for making calls. You might block out 30 minutes in the morning, 30 minutes around lunch time or mid-day, and 30 minutes in the afternoon or evening.

These blocks of time are your "work hours." During those blocks of time you do your most important work: contacting new prospects and following-up with prospects you've already contacted.

You can make significant progress in your business working one hour a day dedicated to these two activities.

During your time blocks, don't take incoming calls, even from prospects calling you back, or calls from your team. Don't let anything else get in the way of doing your most important work.

Other activities—responding to emails, reviewing your notes, listening to a recorded training, talking to your team, listening to team calls, and so on, should be done outside your time blocks. If you want, you can schedule additional time blocks for these secondary activities.

To stay on track for your goals, you might want to share your numbers with your upline or with a "workout partner"—another distributor who is at or near your level and has similar goals to your own.

You can do this during a weekly (or daily) "accountability" call, where you report your goals for the previous week, your actual numbers, and your goals for the coming week. This is an excellent way to make sure you do what you said you would do.

DON'T BREAK THE CHAIN

We say "treat it like a business" but if you've never owned a business, you may not be fully ready to do that. Until you are, the best advice I can give you is to treat your business like a job.

When you are employed, you are accountable to your employer. He or she will notice if you don't show up and do your work. You will be penalized or fired if you don't.

Treating your business like a job means finding ways to hold yourself accountable. Having an accountability partner is one way to do that, but you can also be accountable to yourself.

Look at your daily and weekly schedule. Each day you do what you've planned, note this on your calendar. Did you make your calls? Do your exposures? Do all your follow-ups? If you did, make a mark on your calendar to note that you did it.

Comedian Jerry Seinfeld was once asked how he became so successful. He said that early in his career, he promised himself that no matter what, he would write at least one joke every day. That was something he could do, and he committed to doing it.

Each day, when he completed that task, he would make a big X on his monthly wall calendar. He did this every day and those X's formed a chain. He told himself, "Don't break the chain," meaning don't miss a day, and he didn't.

When you do something every day, you not only get better at doing it, you develop the habit of doing it and that habit eventually delivers your results. Success doesn't happen in a day. It happens when you do the activities every day, over and over, consistently over time. Those little things, such as making calls 30 minutes a day, add up. If you don't break the chain, eventually you find yourself with a sizable team and income.

If you keep the chain going for thirty days, you might reward yourself. Or penalize yourself if you don't.

You might get your spouse or kids involved. Show them your schedule and your "chain" and ask them to hold you accountable.

"Mommy, did you make your calls today?"

Choose a reward that benefits them. For example, tell your kids that if you don't break the chain for two months, you'll take the family to Disneyland or Chuck-E-Cheese or something else they would love and be disappointed if you don't deliver.

Your kids will function like your boss, making sure you don't break the chain.

If you struggle to make all of your calls or other daily activities, it's okay to re-negotiate your schedule with yourself. Many distributors plan more than they can do. If your plan calls for you to make thirty calls a day, for example, and it looks like you can't do this consistently, consider making 15 or 20 calls a day. Or start with 5 calls and build from there.

Do what you can do and keep doing it until you get to where you can consistently do more.

You have a goal—to get to $1,000 per month. Don't focus on the goal, focus on the process. Focus on the activities that will help you reach your goal.

In the last chapter, I talked about the value of a "90-Day Run". I said that's when you run as fast as you can for a solid 90 days, putting as much time and energy into the business as possible.

You talk to everyone on your list, you don't spend time with anyone who's not interested, you follow-up with those who agree to look at some information, and you find some people who want to sign up.

That's what I did when I got started. That's how I earned my first $1,000. And that's how I got to $1,000 per month.

I suggest you do the same. Continue your 90-Day Run, or start another one.

Network marketing is a momentum business. You start from scratch, with no team and no activity. To make something happen, you need to find some people for your team. Not just people willing to sign up but people who are ready to get to work.

If you already have distributors ready to run with you that's great. Work with them, help them, encourage them, and then go get more.

If you don't yet have anyone serious about building the business, trust me, they're out there. You just have to keep running and sorting to find them.

They might be the next prospect you talk to. Or you might sign up five or ten distributors, or more, to find one who is serious.

Don't give up. Don't break the chain. Keep contacting, exposing, and following-up with prospects, and you'll find some who see what you see, want what you want, and are willing to do what you're willing to do to get it.

When you're new, you're learning the basics, developing your skills, making mistakes, and getting into a rhythm. Each prospect you talk to brings you a step closer to reaching your goal.

There's an expression used in many network marketing circles: "Be here a year from now." This is an acknowledgment that your first year will probably be rough and you should commit, in advance, that you will stick around long enough to make things happen.

It happened quickly for me and for others. It might happen quickly for you. But don't count on it. Count on it taking longer than you would like. If it doesn't, great. You'll be ahead of the game. But if it takes longer than you would like, you'll be ready for it.

"Relax and have a career mindset," my friend says. Show up to work every day, stick to your schedule, and have faith that you will get where you want to go.

Chapter 3: Getting to $4,000 per month

Earlier, I talked about the importance of treating your business like a "real" business. Many distributors understand this and attempt to do it. But most of them don't understand what kind of business it is.

If you've read Robert Kiyosaki's "Rich Dad/Poor Dad" books, you've heard him describe four "quadrants" or four basic ways to earn money. The "E" quadrant is Employment. The "S" quadrant refers to Self-Employment or a Small Business. The "I" quadrant refers to Investing. That leaves the "B" quadrant. "B" stands for "Big Business," meaning companies with lots of employees, divisions or groups, and systems to manage everything.

Many distributors believe their network marketing business belongs in the S quadrant because it's a small business. But it's not. A network marketing business is actually in the B (Big Business) quadrant.

Although we don't have lots of employees (or any employees), we have lots of distributors and groups (teams) within our organization, and we run our business with systems.

We start out in the S Quadrant. A new distributor earns all of their income through personal effort. But personal effort can only take you so far. If you want to earn a six-figure or seven-figure passive income, you have to think in terms of owning a big business.

Small businesses and self-employed people—a one-store retailer, a freelancer, a sole practitioner—focus on sales. To increase their income, they have to increase their personal production. A Big Business will do that, too, but the primary way they increase their income is by opening additional units of distribution. They add more retail outlets or franchisees. And that's what we do in network marketing when we recruit more distributors.

We increase our income primarily by recruiting additional distributors and teaching them to duplicate our efforts. As our team grows, it produces more sales volume and we earn bigger overrides.

Like any Big Business, we are system driven. Systems allow new people to come on board and produce quickly. If someone quits or retires, it's easy to replace them. We can open new profit centers in another state or country by recruiting distributors in those countries.

Sure, we want our team to be as productive as possible but we can't expect our distributors to become better at sales, something most of them don't want to do. We can, however, teach them how to make a few sales and find a few distributors who make a few sales, and duplicate this throughout our organization.

In some network marketing companies, distributors can earn a healthy income through sales. That might because they sell big-ticket products with large commissions, or a product or service that can be sold in quantity to companies or organizations or other groups. The distributor might have a sales background and a lot of contacts or customers they can go back to. That's all good. But the big money in network marketing is in recruiting, not sales.

No matter how good you are, you'll never be able to sell as much as a team. To earn a full-time income from your business and not do everything yourself, focus on recruiting.

Top money-earners focus on the business opportunity, not the products. In fact, unless a prospect tells you about a problem or concern they have that can be addressed by one of your products or services, you should talk to them first about the business.

Lead with the business; fall back on the product. If a prospect isn't interested in the business, they may still buy your product. If a prospect isn't interested in your product, however, they are probably unlikely to be interested in the business.

Some distributors prefer to lead with their product. They show their product or service to prospects and when the prospect buys the product, they show them the business. That works, but it's a slower process. You'll grow faster if you focus on recruiting, not sales.

The quickest way to build your business is to recruit people who want to build a team and make a lot of money. Yes, you also want thousands of people who love your products and share them with their friends, but it the business builders who will build a big organization.

In the end, you want to show both the product and the business to everyone and let them decide. But if you want to build your business quickly, focus on recruiting.

FINDING PROSPECTS—GOING BEYOND THE WARM MARKET

To go from $1,000 per month to $4,000 per month most distributors need to go beyond their warm market. If you're still working your warm market, congratulations. Stay with it. It's easier than the cold market.

Eventually, you'll need to (or want to) venture into the cold market. But between the warm market and the cold market are referrals.

As you work your way through your warm market, develop the habit of asking everyone for referrals. These can be referrals for your products or the business opportunity. (You're looking for business builders but sometimes it's easier to get referrals for your products).

Here are some ways to ask:

"Who do you know who might want [some benefits offered by your product(s)]"

"I know you know a lot of people at work—who do you know who might want to get a free sample of [product]?"

"I build my business through referrals. It would mean a lot to me if you would give me a few names of people I could talk to. Could you help me out?"

"I'll bet you know some people who have been in network marketing/want to work from home/would like to earn some extra income. Could you give me a couple of names?"

"Who do you know who might be interested in developing a second source of income or possibly start a new career?"

"I work with a lot of stay-at-home moms and showing them how to earn extra income from home. Who do you know I should talk to?"

"I work with a lot of real estate agents. Who do you know who might want to take a look at what we do?"

Most people won't give you referrals unless you ask for them. So ask.

People will provide referrals because they love your products and want others to have the benefits they're getting. Some will provide referrals because they want to help you start or grow your business. And some will provide referrals simply because you asked.

You've got nothing to lose by asking. So ask everyone for referrals.

Then, when a referral buys something or signs up as a distributor, go back to the person who referred them, thank them again, and ask them if they want to earn the commission. Tell them you'll give them the sale or put the distributor who just signed up under them so they can get the commissions or overrides. Tell them how much they'll get or how excited the new distributor is and how well you think they'll do in the business.

You'd be surprised at how many people will change their mind and sign up as a distributor when one of their referrals signs up.

As you sign up distributors and ask them to make a list, get in the habit of asking for a copy of that list. Tell them it will make it easier for you to help them contact their prospects, and it will. But if your new distributor doesn't contact them, you can do it. If any of them sign up, go back to your distributor and let them know they have a sale or a new distributor on their team.

That's often enough to get the distributor to "wake up" and get going.

If those prospects don't buy or sign up as a distributor, you can ask them for referrals, too.

If you get good at asking for referrals, you may never run out of people to talk to.

GETTING STARTED IN THE COLD MARKET

Everywhere you go where there are people there is an opportunity to strike up a conversation and make a new contact. Some of those new contacts will become customers. Some of them will join you in the business. Some will provide referrals.

You might meet people through social media. Start a conversation with them online. When the time is right, talk to them on the phone.

You might meet people through formal networking groups in your area. There are thousands of groups you can join or visit—business networking groups, hobby-related groups, community groups, and many more.

Prospects are everywhere. Meet a few new people every day. Get their contact information and add it to your list.

If you want to go faster, you can buy leads. These are lists of people who have expressed interest in working from home, starting a business, or earning extra income. You can also buy lists of people who have been a network marketing distributor.

Ask your upline if they can recommend a company that sells "business opportunity" (biz opp) leads. Many lead companies (and teams who use them) have training calls. You can dial and listen to other distributors talking to prospects. You'll hear how they open the conversation, find out what the prospect is looking for, get them to look at some information about your company, and schedule a follow-up.

You can also create your own leads. If you're interested in doing that at some point, check out my book, *5-Minute Recruiting: Using Voicemail to Build Your Network Marketing Business.*

MORE WAYS TO FIND PROSPECTS

I've done a lot of cold calling to build my business. You may not think it's your cup of tea but withhold judgment until you've tried it. It is especially effective if you want to recruit professionals, something I do almost exclusively. My book, *Recruiting Up* shows you how to do that, as well as other ways to find and recruit professionals.

Many network marketers recruit online through social media. You can search via keywords or groups and find people who are interested in business opportunities, or people who share an interest in something related to what you offer.

Those are just a few ways to find cold market prospects. As you develop your skills, you'll find additional lead generation methods that work best for you.

The cold market is more challenging than the warm market but it is unlimited. You will never run out of people to talk to.

WORKING WITH YOUR CUSTOMERS

One of the best ways to increase your income is to increase customer retention. Get your customers to order again, buy other products, and increase the average size of their orders. It will be well worth your effort. Even a small percentage increase in your overall retention numbers could cause a significant increase in your income.

It is far easier to get an existing customer to re-order than to get a prospective customer to place their first order. The existing customer knows and trusts you. If they got benefits from your products, it shouldn't take much more than a reminder from you to get them to order again.

It's also relatively easy to get an existing customer to try another one of your products. Get them the information, and perhaps a sample, or tell them about your "risk free" offer, and many will say yes.

Find out if your company has any incentives you can offer to encourage customers to try new products, reward them for signing up for auto-ship or place a bigger order. Even something like free shipping may get customers to try something new. These incentives are also useful for bringing in new customers.

Your company should have information or training to help you increase retention and sales. Find out what they have and use it.

Good retention begins at the time of the first sale. Don't promise results your products can't deliver. In fact, it's better to under-promise so your products can over-deliver.

You want to get prospective customers excited about what your products can do for them but not so excited that they expect better results or faster results than they are likely to get. Your sales tools will do a lot of this for you, but talk to your customers and prospects and make sure they have reasonable expectations before you take their order.

No matter how good you are at servicing your customers, a significant percentage will fall off. They may order once and never again. They may re-order for a few months and stop. They may be loyal customers for many years and suddenly disappear.

There are many reasons why a customer might stop ordering. They might not see the results they expected. They might be seduced by a lower-cost competitor. They may no longer be able to afford your products. Or they may no longer need what you sell.

It happens in every business. You can't avoid it. Do your best to minimize these losses and maximize orders from customers who stick with you.

Lapsed customers do come back. Maybe your customer will try a lower-priced product and be unhappy with the results and be open to buying your products again. Go back to lapsed customers and talk to them. Find out why they stopped ordering.

Maybe they ran out and didn't realize they hadn't re-ordered. Maybe they had a money issue and didn't know they could buy a smaller size or a less expensive version. If they didn't get the benefits they wanted with product A, perhaps they will get benefits with product B.

Increasing sales and retention often comes down to more frequent communication with your customers. Check in with them regularly to see if your products are still meeting their needs and if they have questions or complaints.

When a customer is unhappy, address it immediately. Find out what's wrong and do what you have to do to fix it. Be prepared to offer them an incentive, e.g., a free product or discount, as a "peace offering" and to get them to try again.

Develop a system for staying in touch with all your customers. Spending a few minutes each day emailing and calling customers will be well worth your time.

Send them information about new products, special offers, testimonials, and important company or industry news. Tell them how you're doing in the business, or how someone they know is doing in the business. Every time they hear from you it is another opportunity to remind them about the problems your products solve and opportunities your business offers.

You should also do that with prospects—people who looked at some information and decided not to become a distributor or customer. You never know when someone who wasn't interested or wasn't ready in the past might be ready to do something today. I've mentioned that I've signed up distributors many years after I first spoke to them. Keep your name and message in front of your prospects and you will, too.

When a customer tells you they're happy with the products, ask for a testimonial and referrals. "Who do you know who might want to get some information about xyz [and/or a free sample]?" If you can, offer them referral fees or coupons they can use to re-order at a discount.

You should also talk to them about the business. Satisfied customers are a great source of new distributors. They use the products and are happy with them. They're probably telling their friends and family about them anyway. They might as well get paid.

If you've shown them the business before and they said no, they might give you a different answer today. Keep in touch with all of your prospects and customers. When things change and they're ready to join your business, you'll be on their mind and in their mailbox, just a click or a phone call away.

Finally, teach your team what you're doing to increase retention and sales and help them do the same thing with their customers.

WORKING WITH YOUR TEAM

Working with new distributors means helping new distributors get their business started. You'll do this for distributors you recruit and, sometimes, for distributors recruited by your team when you want to show their sponsor what to do.

Working with new distributors means doing things like:

- Conducting their game plan (setting goals, going over their list, making sure they set up their website, talking to them about the tools, the local training and events, etc.) A game plan could be anywhere from 45 minutes to two hours.
- Helping them invite prospects to an event and/or do their first exposures. You coach them on what to say and/or listen to them while they make calls. Sometimes, you'll have them introduce you to a few prospects and listen while you invite them to come to an event, watch a video, or visit the distributor's website.

- Helping them conduct a launch event (e.g., home party, conference call) if your team does these. You tell your story, share a video or recorded message or do the presentation, answer questions, overcome objections, and close the prospects or invite them to take the next step. A well-attended launch event may produce enough sales and recruits for the new distributor to get their first promotion.
- Talking to their interested prospects via 3-way call, to answer questions, overcome objections, and close.
- Helping them do the game plan with their first few distributors.
- Being available to answer questions about the business.

You learn how to do these things primarily by watching your sponsor or upline do them for you and/or your new distributors and attending training.

That's how I learned. That's how you will learn. And remember, until you're able to do it yourself, you can call on your upline for help.

At some point, you may do your own team calls. You might start with a few of your leaders, or a few distributors who want to be leaders. You provide training, share tips and success stories, promote upcoming events, and recognize your team's progress. If you're still relatively new, you invite your upline or other leaders to be your guest speaker.

You'll also learn

- How to edify and introduce your upline, the speaker or trainer at the events, and other distributors, in a way that makes your prospects or distributors respect and value them.
- How to promote events so you get more people attending. Network marketing is an event-driven business and the more "butts in seats" you have on your team—guests and distributors—the better. You'll also learn how to promote the company and/or team contests, trips, and other incentives, to get distributors on your team working towards them.
- How to do welcome calls. Your team will get you on the phone with their new distributors (or introduce you at an event). You welcome them to the team, tell them your story, offer to help them, and promote the next event.
- How to praise and recognize distributors for things like bringing guests to the events, getting a new distributor, getting their first promotion, and so on. Show them (and the rest of your team who hears you do this) that they are doing well and you are excited for their progress.
- How to conduct a circle-up with your team and their prospects and then close the prospects, recognize your team's successes, and promote the next event.

You'll learn these by watching your upline and others do them.

At the end of an event, for example, you and your guests will "circle up" with your upline and listen to them answer questions, close, and promote the next event.

You'll learn how to do 3-way calls as an "expert" by doing 3-way calls to your upline with your guests and listening to them answer questions.

At some point, you may want to run your own promotions, e.g., providing a small prize to the top recruiter on your team for the week or month.

It may sound like a lot to learn and do but it really isn't. Keep going to training, keep getting on conference calls, and keep signing up distributors and helping them get started and you'll be able to do all of this, and more, without thinking about it.

I didn't know how to do any of this when I got started. I learned everything by working the business, going to events, and observing my upline. Such is the power of network marketing.

As your team grows, you'll want to identify leaders and future leaders. They are the ones who are treating it like a business. They do daily exposures, they get on all the calls and come to all the events, they get you on the phone to speak to their prospects and welcome their new distributors. They have a good attitude and work ethic. They show you that they have the desire to succeed, they are teachable, and they are willing to work.

And they are getting results.

These are your leaders and future leaders.

Once you've identified them, focus on them. If their team is growing, help them grow it bigger and faster. If they're earning money, help them earn more. Don't ignore the rest of your team but the best use of your time with your team is to work with the ones who are "doing it".

Work with the willing. Work with the ones who deserve your help.

You may only have a few but remember, a few is all you need. With your help, they will find a few leaders and duplicate what they've learned from you and others and as their teams grow, so will yours.

KEEP YOUR FOOT ON THE GAS

Getting to $1,000 per month is a significant accomplishment. You own a real business that's producing real income. A good portion of that income may still be coming from your own efforts but that's about to change.

You have a team now. Help them get to $1,000 per month, and the increase in their production will help you get to $4,000 per month.

Work with customers, work with your team, and continue your own recruiting. You'll need new distributors to replace the ones who quit or run out of steam and to create new legs and new profit centers for your growing business.

At this point, you may want to put more time into the business. A little bit can go a long way. If you've been working 60 minutes a day, see if you can increase that to 90 minutes.

At first, you might put in more time but not see a commensurate increase in results. That's normal. Give it time. Just as it takes time for you to find some serious distributors, it takes time for them to learn the business and find a few serious distributors of their own.

Keep going. The results will come.

Sadly, many people quit network marketing just before their business was about to take off. They couldn't see it coming. They thought they had gone as far as they can go. Life gets in the way.

Don't let that happen to you.

When you got started, you worked hard and may not have seen the results you were after. But then you did.

The same thing happens at every stage. You do the work without seeing much happening, and one day you reach a tipping point. You achieve momentum and your business takes off.

Decide now that no matter what, no matter how long it takes, you won't quit.

Don't take your foot off the gas. Keep driving and you will eventually get where you want to go.

Chapter 4: Getting to $10,000 per month (and beyond)

When you're earning $4,000 per month, primarily from team overrides, you are much closer to $10,000 than you realize.

$10,000 is two-and-a-half times $4,000, which seems like a long way off, but it's easier to go from $4,000 to $10,000 per month than to go from zero to $1,000 per month.

That's because you have leaders on your team now, and up-and-coming leaders, who are producing for you (via overrides) a significant percentage of your income. As they build their teams, they do most of the work, freeing you up to recruit new legs and create new profit centers.

In other words, $4,000 of your income is nearly entirely passive *and will continue to grow without you.*

And, the overrides you earn on new legs you build will be greater than the overrides you earn on legs with established leaders in them.

Let's say you are earning an average override of $10 on each sale in your established legs. If those legs do 400 sales per month, you're earning $4,000 per month on those legs (plus bonuses, if any).

On your new legs, your distributors earn less, because they at a lower level in the comp plan. Generally, you earn overrides based on the difference between what they earn at their level and what you earn at your higher level. (Check your comp plan for the details.)

If you start a few new legs and help them build up a volume of 100 sales and you earn $50 per sale in overrides, you'll earn $5,000 on those new legs. That plus the overrides on your other legs, plus your own personal sales, and bonuses, will bring you close to earning $10,000 per month.

You're also closer than you think because you are more skilled than you were when you started. You also have more confidence and a more compelling story, all of which means you should be able to recruit more quickly and easily.

You are also closer to earning $10,000 than you think because your team is now compounding. Before, your team grew primarily by addition. You were doing most of the recruiting and you added new distributors one at a time. Now, many distributors are recruiting and your team (and income) is growing by multiplication.

MY JOURNEY TO A SIX-FIGURE INCOME

As you know, I got to $4,000 per month in less than six months. In my first full year I earned $17,500. I worked only a few hours a week and was pleased with that. I could see that the business was working, and I was confident I could do better. I kept working (and put in a little more time) and in my second year my income tripled to $53,000.

Most of that was from overrides. And yes, I was still part time.

I kept going and in my third year I earned $82,000. In my fourth year, my income dropped to $70,000. Why? I took my foot off the gas, thinking I would continue to grow as quickly as I had been growing. When I didn't, it motivated me to work harder and the next year I passed the six-figure mark.

I thought I'd get there much sooner, but I was happy. I earned much more in my law practice, but earning a six-figure passive income (with no employees and minimal overhead), showed me that this business could provide me with the freedom I wanted.

I can't tell you how long it will take you to get to a six-figure income. It will take as long as it takes.

You'll know you're getting close when it seems like the days are flying by, you're constantly busy, often exhausted, and you can't seem to keep up with everything.

You're on the phone most of the day, you're going to lots of events, new people are joining your organization daily and you don't know who they are or who recruited them, your numbers are doubling and tripling, and one day, you stop and take inventory and realize that you've had your first $10,000 month.

Let's talk about what to do to make that happen.

WHY SOME GROW BIGGER, FASTER

Every distributor in your company has the same products, the same comp plan, and the same tools. Why do some distributors earn more and build a bigger business? Why do their teams grow faster?

Sometimes, they work harder than others.

Sometimes, they get lucky and find a few leaders early in their career.

Sometimes, it's because they have previous network marketing experience. They already knew what to do and could start doing it immediately. They also know many other people with network marketing experience, many of whom join their team and recruit other network marketers.

Don't compare yourself to these people. They spent years in network marketing and if you haven't done that, you can't expect to do what they can do.

But you can recruit them.

Most network marketing trainers recommend targeting people with network marketing experience. I agree. Some trainers say we should *only* recruit people with network marketing experience. I won't go that far.

I built a successful business without targeting people with network marketing experience. I know many others who have done that, too.

I recruited professionals, business owners, and other influential people with a big warm market. My business grew bigger and faster because I recruited a lot of people who recruited a lot of people. I suggest you do the same. (See *Recruiting Up*.)

You don't have to recruit professionals but I suggest you specialize. Choose one or more niche markets and spend most of your time recruiting prospects in those markets. When you specialize, you get better at recruiting prospects in those niches.

If you have a background in real estate sales, for example, focus on recruiting real estate brokers and agents. It makes sense. You understand the industry. You speak the same "language". You relate to them and they relate to you. It's easier to recruit someone when they know you're "one of them," especially when they find out you already have twenty other real estate agents on your team.

I specialize in recruiting attorneys. Attorneys relate to me and my story. I know their challenges and desires, I know how to talk to them, and I can recruit them more easily than I can recruit people with a different background.

On the other hand, many distributors don't have a background in the niche markets they specialize in. You don't need to be a physician to recruit physicians into your health-based business.

Sure, it's better if you are but it's almost as effective to point to the other physicians on your team or with the company.

Many leaders don't specialize. They say "recruit everyone"—you never know who will build a big business or lead you to someone who does. "Quantity leads to quality." That's true. People you recruit will lead you to the professionals, business owners, network marketers, and other influential people in their warm market.

But you find a lot more of them when you recruit them yourself.

One thing is clear—you can't sign up three or four distributors and expect to build a six-figure income. The odds are against you. Successful distributors sign up dozens of distributors, and some sign up many more.

I've recruited hundreds of distributors. While it's true that many network marketers recruit fewer and earn more than I do, if you want to earn a six-figure income, I suggest you plan on recruiting as many distributors as possible.

DEVELOPING AS A LEADER

When I started in network marketing I had no idea how to work with a team. I was used to having employees and telling them what to do. Network marketing is different.

Nobody works for you. Nobody has to do anything you say. Everyone in your organization is in business for themselves.

In the beginning, I lost distributors by pushing them and telling them what they "should" do. I hadn't learned the difference between leading a team and managing employees.

Leadership is influence. It's about getting people to do things by helping them to see why it's in their best interest to do so. It's about raising people up and helping them realize their potential, and guiding them and supporting them on their journey.

You show them what's possible and encourage them, but you let them go at their own pace. Then, you run with the runners and walk with the walkers. If someone wants to sit in the stands and watch the race instead of taking part in it, you leave them alone, but let them know you're ready to help them when they're ready to get going.

I eventually learned how to be a leader and it made a big difference in the growth of my business. As you move to the six-figure income level, one of your top priorities is to develop as a leader.

I learned how to grow into a leader by spending time with leaders in my company and listening to how they spoke to their team. I asked lots of questions and took lots of notes. I watched them praise distributors when they did something right, instead of what I had been doing—pushing them and pointing out what they did wrong.

I learned about leadership by paying attention to what my upline mentor said to me—how he encouraged me and told me that I was going all the way in the business. When I was discouraged, his words picked me up and kept me going. When I was excited, he kept me from getting cocky and lazy.

I learned about leadership by going to all the training events offered by my company and my upline organization. I got on every conference call, went to every convention, read every book and watched every video on leadership I could find.

But I learned the most about leadership by working with my team.

I inspired them by painting verbal pictures of the better future that lie ahead for them. I shared stories about my upline, about other distributors on the team, and about myself—telling them about our challenges and how we overcame them and about our goals and how we achieved them. I made them feel good about themselves and let them know that I was ready to help them every step of the way. And I set an example for them by continuing to recruit and build my business.

I did with my team what my upline had done with me.

GET TO KNOW YOUR PEOPLE

As you get to know the individuals on your team, find out what they want and show them how the business can help them get it.

Some distributors are motivated by money and power. Talk them about commissions, bonuses, overrides, and what they can do with the money they earn. Talk to them about being recognized on stage, about moving up the comp plan, and about qualifying to attend the "executive dinner" and sit with other leaders.

Some distributors love helping people. Talk to them about the company's cause and how it is making the world a better place. Share success stories about the people who have improved their lives by using the products or services and helping others get involved in the business. Remind them that what they do is important and valuable. Talk to them about how they are a part of something big and they can help to make it bigger.

Some distributors love to have fun. Talk to them about the team events, the parties, the trips, and all the cool people on the team. Talk to them about being able to work with their friends and recruit more of them. Talk to them about the food, the music, and the laughter.

Some distributors love being able to work with a company that's doing things right. Talk to them about the financial strength and reputation of the company, the integrity of the founder and executives, the third-party credibility (endorsements, awards, accolades, etc.), the high-quality products or services, and how smart they are for choosing to align with this first-class company.

When you talk to your team in a group setting, you'll want to touch on all of these areas so you can appeal to everyone in your group. When you speak to individuals on your team, use language they can relate to. If you're talking to someone who is motivated by money, for example, challenge them to get to the next level. If you're talking to someone motivated by working with a company that's doing things right, encourage them to find like-minded people and introduce them to the opportunity.

As you get to know the people on your team, you'll learn what's important to them. You'll learn their "why". If they are building this business so they can have more time with their family, for example, talk about that, remind them about that, especially when they are going through a tough time.

Get to know your distributor's family and introduce them to yours. Many people on my team relate to my wife much more than they relate to me.

Spend time with your team. They are your business partners and your future. When you build a relationship with them, they'll stick with you when they might otherwise think about quitting. You'll get to know when they need help and when they want to be left alone, when they need a pat on the back, advice, or a hug.

We are in the people business and our team is our greatest asset.

THE LAW OF THE LID

Leaders set the pace for their organization. "The speed of the leader is the speed of the pack," it is said. In *The 21 Irrefutable Laws of Leadership,* John C. Maxwell's first law of leadership is "The Law of the Lid". The leader's lid is his or her maximum ability to lead.

Your lid determines the potential of your team.

If your leadership ability is a 4 on a scale of 1 to 10, your team's potential will never be more than a 3. If you increase your leadership ability to an 8 or 9, the team's potential will increase to a 7 or 8.

You can increase your effectiveness as a leader (raise your lid) by learning how to provide more value to your team, to prospects looking at joining your organization, and to other leaders in the company.

Helping your team is obvious. What may not be as obvious is the idea of helping people who aren't in your organization. The more you do that, the more you learn about leadership, how to solve problems and inspire people, and the more you grow as a leader.

Adding value can take many forms:

- Sharing what you've learned on team calls and/or on stage
- Inspiring distributors with your story, e.g., providing a testimonial at an event or on a call, and sharing stories you've learned from others
- Helping new distributors do a game plan, set goals, conduct a launch event
- Coaching people who need guidance
- Promoting other leaders' events
- Edifying distributors to their prospects, team, and upline
- Doing 3-way calls for the prospects of distributors on other teams
- Being a guest speaker at other team's events and on their team calls

- Holding a distributor's hand when they are struggling, giving them a high-five when they are doing well

As you help other leaders and their teams, you find they are inclined to help you and your team. I often do 3-way calls for distributors in other organizations, especially when their prospects are attorneys. I talk to their prospects, tell them my story, answer questions, and encourage them to sign up in the business. If they have signed up, I welcome them, tell them my story, tell them about other attorneys in the company, and offer them some tips and encouragement.

In return, other leaders talk to my prospects or prospects for distributors on my team. If someone on my team has a prospect who is a school teacher, for example, I'll introduce them to a school teacher on my team.

What you give you get. Yes, The Golden Rule is alive and well in network marketing.

LEAD YOUR TEAM, DON'T "BABY" THEM

Some distributors behave like "helicopter parents," hovering over their distributors, guarding them from danger. They are overprotective and don't allow their distributors to make mistakes or figure things out for themselves. They mean well but they breed weak and dependent "children" who never seem to grow up.

A common example of babying your team is saving seats for them at the events. Don't do that. Tell them to leave home early enough to get to the event on time.

Another example is sharing your notes with your team. If you do that, the message you send is that they don't need to take notes, they don't even have to go the training because they can get the notes from you.

Instead of saving seats and sharing notes, promote the training event so they know why they need to be there. Teach them why it's important to be at the events and show up on time. Make sure they understand that their team need to see them at the event or they won't go. And make sure they see you at the events, in the front row, paying attention, laughing at the speaker's jokes (even though you've heard them 100 times before) and taking notes.

Teach your team what to do and trust them to do it. Let them mess up.

When they fall down, be there to pick them up. Give them a hug and encourage them to try again.

When they're ready, push them out of the nest and let them fly on their own.

DON'T RE-INVENT THE WHEEL

In network marketing, your goal is "to get a large number of people to do a few simple things, consistently, over time." If you want to build a large organization with thousands of distributors, most of whom you don't know and will never meet, you have to follow and teach the same system you want them to follow.

Your team learns that system at trainings and by watching you and other distributors faithfully follow that system.

The problem is, when you do the same things over and over again, things can get boring. There's a natural tendency to want to change things.

Don't do it. Don't make your own tools or websites. Don't introduce new methods or trainings. Don't teach your team new ways to build the business.

If the system is working, don't change it. It got you where you are and it will get you to the next level.

If you change things, even a little, you confuse your team. "Should I do it this way or the other way? Should I use this approach or the first one I learned? Should I invite prospects to hear the usual recorded message or the new one I heard about?"

When you confuse your team, they slow down and go in different directions. Some of your team will do it one way, some do something else, and some introduce their own changes.

Duplication comes to a screeching halt.

You may be bored with the system but your prospects and new distributors are seeing it for the first time. They're not bored, they're excited.

Stick with the approaches and methods and tools they taught you, at least until you've been around long enough and have had enough success to know when it might be okay to change something or add another element.

But think twice before you do that.

CREATE LEADERS, NOT FOLLOWERS

Marcus Buckingham, author of *The One Thing You Need to Know: ... About Great Managing, Great Leading, and Sustained Individual Success,* says leaders are never satisfied with the status quo. "What defines a leader is his preoccupation with the future. In his head he carries a vivid image of what the future could be, and this image drives him on. This image, rather than, say, goals of outperforming competitors, or being individually productive, or helping others achieve success, is what motivates the leader."

It's not that you don't want to be better than the competition or help people. It's that you feel compelled to take your business to the next level and doing whatever you need to do to make that happen. When you share your vision of the future, your team hears you talk about this bigger and better future and wants to join you on your journey.

When I got to a certain point in my business, I broke away from my upline. I gave my team a name, set up a website, and started my own team calls. My upline had all that going, but I wanted to take ownership of my business and take my team where I wanted to take it. I wanted to run my business instead of merely plugging into what my upline was doing.

I was doing what Buckingham says all leaders do:

"The key thing about leading is not only that you envision a better future, but also that you believe, in every fiber of your being, that you are the one to make this future come true. You are the one to assume the responsibility for transforming the present into something better. From all my interviews with effective leaders I cannot think of one example in which the person lacked this craving to be at the helm, charting the course ahead."

If your upline organization is doing things consistent with the future you envision, stick with them. Promote their training and events and take part in them. But if you feel that something is missing, or you feel compelled to chart your own course, consider starting your own team.

Leaders realize that there is no success without successors. They want to build a team of leaders, not followers. And they want their leaders to get big enough and strong enough and skilled enough to break away and start their own trainings and events.

Just as you want your children to leave home and start their own family, you want your network marketing children to go out on their own. You help them get started, you teach them what to do and how to do it, and you support them while they do it. Eventually, they know what to do and don't need your help. But like your children who move out on their own, they know that if they ever need help or advice, you'll be there for them.

That's what allows you to build a business that provides you with true passive income. It's what allows you to retire someday, knowing your business will continue to operate and grow without you.

Chapter 5: What it REALLY takes to reach the top

Everyone makes it look easy, don't they? All those excited people telling you how excited they are. All those stories about money, cars, trips, free time, and fun.

They tell you how they were broke and desperate and had never owned a business. They tell you they signed up and followed the system they were taught and within a few months they could quit their job, work from home, and completely change their life.

They're telling you the truth. What's they're not telling you is how hard they worked to make it happen.

They don't tell you about the rejection they got from people they were sure would sign up but didn't. They don't tell you about all the time they spent inviting people to events, doing the exposures and follow-ups, and working with their team.

They worked hard but they want you to think it's easy. It's not. And most people don't achieve what they achieved.

When I started in the business, I knew most people would say no. I was prepared for that. I expected to hear a lot of noes on my way to finding the ones who said yes.

What I didn't expect was that most of the people who say "yes" (and sign up) do little or nothing.

Eighty percent or more who sign up never get trained, never make a list, and never talk to anyone about their products or business.

And that's why most people make little or nothing in network marketing.

I didn't get it. Why would anyone sign up and do nothing? Why would distributors who told me they were excited not get to work?

I talked to a leader in our company, shared my numbers, and asked him for advice.

He said what I was seeing was normal and confirmed that most distributors do little or nothing.

I was relieved to learn that it was normal (and not my fault!) but I couldn't understand something. *How do you build a successful business if most people do little or nothing?*

His answer changed my life. He said, "You only need a few."

You only need a few who are serious and committed to building the business. You help them find a few, repeat the process, and through the magic of compounding you can grow a big team. A few committed people duplicate and grow into thousands.

And then he told me about his numbers. He had many thousands of distributors on his team and most of them had zeros next to their name. Only a small percentage were working but they did enough business to earn him six-figures in overrides.

"Why don't you tell this to new distributors when they get started?" He said they don't want to scare off anyone. If new distributors knew most people do nothing, they might decide to join them.

This didn't scare me, it excited me. Most people do little or nothing and you can still build a big business!

DON'T WISH IT WAS EASY

Okay, it takes a lot of hard work to build a successful network marketing business. Guess what? Every business takes a lot of hard work. Why should network marketing be different?

If it was easy, your company wouldn't need you. They'd sell their products or services through advertising or through the Internet. They need you (and will pay you a lot of money) because they can't do that or because they can earn more by paying you and other distributors to do it for them.

They need distributors to build the market. They need distributors to recruit and train other distributors and build a large distributor organization.

So, be thankful that it's hard. Because if it was easy, there would be no opportunity for you.

On the other hand, "hard" is relative. I've started several "traditional" businesses. I've started and built a successful law practice from scratch. Lots of blood, sweat and tears. That's hard work.

Compared to building a traditional business or a professional practice, building a network marketing business is easy.

Where else can you talk on the phone for a few hours a day and make the money we make? Where else can you invest a few years and build a six-figure *passive* income that gives you time freedom and retirement income?

I didn't know of anything else. That's why, although I had other options, I started a network marketing business.

HOW TO OVERCOME FEAR AND PROCRASTINATION

Starting a business requires you to do things you haven't done before. It forces you to get out of your comfort zone. Arguably, this is the most difficult part of building a business.

Whether it's making your first few calls, conducting your first team training, or doing any other part of the business, there are things you can do to overcome your fears and doubts, or do what you need to do despite them. And if you want to succeed, you must.

You can get more training. You can practice. You can get coaching from your upline, or have them come with you as you take your first steps.

Ultimately, you have to do the things you fear. Mark Twain said, "Do the thing you fear most and the death of fear is certain." Dale Carnegie put it this way: "Inaction breeds doubt and fear. Action breeds confidence and courage. If you want to conquer fear, do not sit home and think about it. Go out and get busy."

I know, that's easier said than done.

But once you start (and your worst fears don't occur), it's easier to keep going. You might sweat bullets before you make the first few calls but once you get them done, the next few are much easier. Eventually, your fears will probably be long gone. You'll laugh at how you felt when you were getting started.

One thing that can help is called "the five-minute rule". Whatever scares you or you'd like to avoid, do it for just five minutes.

You can do anything for five minutes. Five minutes and you're done. Do it and reward yourself with a big hunk of chocolate cake or something just as tasty.

If five minutes is too difficult, do one minute. Or thirty seconds.

Starting is the hardest part and also the most important. If you start, you can continue. In fact, once you do five minutes, you'll probably want to do another five minutes. And another.

If you still have trouble getting started, you can use "the five-second rule".

Here's how it works.

If you're making calls, get some names and numbers ready. Then, do a five-second countdown—five, four, three, two, one, and dial the first number. Don't think about it, just do it. Five, four, three, two, one—dial.

That's what I do when I have a call I don't want to make. It doesn't happen often, but it happens. Even after all these years.

Try the five-minute rule and the five-second rule and the death of your fears is certain.

HOW TO SPEED UP YOUR JOURNEY

When I got started in network marketing, I knew I had some skills I could use, I certainly had the desire, I was willing to work hard, and I believed in the company and the products. But as I mentioned earlier, I didn't know if I had what it takes to succeed in network marketing.

I joke about it sometimes when I'm telling my story. "As an attorney, I argued with people for a living. I found out that network marketing is different. You actually have to be nice to people."

But I believed in myself and that was enough to start.

If you believe you have the talent to build a big business, you will approach the work with a different attitude than someone who doubts it. If you believe in yourself and the first 50 prospects you contact say no, you'll be able to shrug it off and keep going.

To make it to the top you have to think big and believe you can get to the top. If you don't believe it's possible for you won't do what you need to do to get there.

Fortunately, you can change your beliefs. It takes time to do that but you can start immediately. As Jim Rohn said, "You can't change your destination overnight. But you can change your direction overnight."

And you can begin seeing improved results sooner than you might think.

THE LAW OF ASSOCIATION

One way to acquire the belief you need is to "act as if" you have it.

If you doubt your ability to recruit professionals, for example, ask yourself, "What would I think, say, and do if I believed I could do that?" If you doubt your ability to speak on stage (and you want to), find out what someone with that ability thinks, says, and does.

Then, think, say, and do those things.

Yes, pretend. Fake it until you make it.

I know, this may sound silly but there is scientific evidence that "acting as if" can help you become the kind of person you want to become.

If you're not confident, act confident. Continue doing that and eventually you will be confident. If you're not someone who likes meeting new people, figure out what someone who likes meeting new people is like and act like them.

Whatever you lack, you can acquire. And, you're in luck. There are many people in your upline and elsewhere in the company you can learn from and model.

Spend time with the leaders in your company—the speakers, trainers, top recruiters, top producers and top money-earners. Sit near them at the events. Go with them to the after-events. Ask them what books they recommend and read them. Watch their body language, listen to the way they speak, study their habits and do what they do.

Keep doing that and you will eventually become like them. It's called The Law of Association—you become like the people you associate with most.

I met and spent time with the leaders in our company, hearing their stories, listening to their tips, watching them work with their teams. More than anything, this caused my belief level to go way up. As I got to know them, I could see I could do what they had done.

But beware. The Law of Association can also work against you. If you associate with people with bad habits, negative ideas, and poor behavior, you will become like them, too.

Look at the people in your life who don't have what you want and don't do what you want to do and disassociate from them. Stop hanging out with negative people—replace them with positive, success-oriented people like the person you want to become.

I'm not the person I was when I began my network marketing journey. By immersing myself in the business, associating with the leaders, and acting as if I was the leader I wanted to become, my belief grew, and I developed into the leader I became.

THE BEST ADVICE MY UPLINE GAVE ME

One of the best ways to build your belief is to attend the conventions and other big events. I went to all of them because they told me that's where the top people go.

At the conventions, you see the big picture. You hear from top money-earners, corporate executives, and others, who share their vision for the future of the company. You hear news, stories, and training you usually don't get at your local events. You get to associate with the leaders, learn from them, and build relationships with them.

Conventions are one of the best ways to build your belief in your company and your future.

I've seen countless distributors who were discouraged and ready to give up turn around and build a successful business because of what they saw at a convention. They often had to borrow the money to go. They may have had to "call in sick" at work to get the time off. They had every excuse to not go but someone in their upline believed in them enough to convince them to go. I know that most of them would tell you that going was the absolute best thing they ever did.

I've seen many distributors go from "not much" to "blowing up" all because they went to a convention.

AVOID POLITICS

Sometimes, you meet other distributors who spend lots of time chatting (complaining, gossiping, questioning) the company or their upline. They get caught up in politics and fall out of production.

When you spend your time focused on politics, listening to rumors and spreading them to others, all you do is destroy belief. Don't do that. Keep your head down, ignore all the behind-the-scenes nonsense, and stay focused on building your business.

If there's bad news, bring it to your upline, never to your downline. Teach your team to bring their challenges, questions, and issues to you or your upline and not to share it with their team.

Bad news travels up. Good news travels down.

One responsibility of a leader is to show their team their vision of the better future that awaits them through the business. Your upline should show you that future and protect you from the politics that might distract you and knock you off track. You should do the same for your team.

YOU'RE ONLY ONE RECRUIT AWAY FROM AN EXPLOSION

One day, when you least expect it, you or someone on your team will recruit someone who will build a huge business.

Stick around long enough and it is inevitable.

When it happens, no matter where you are in the business, it will change you. You'll see what this superstar is doing and how quickly their team is growing and you'll get excited. Your belief level will skyrocket.

If you've been struggling up to that point, you'll realize that the business really works. It will be a turning point for you and you'll work harder and accomplish more than you have before because your belief will have gone way up.

It's important to know this now, before it happens, because it will keep you in the business, working and building, because you know what lies ahead and you want to be there when it happens. You won't want to miss all that growth and all those overrides.

WHATEVER IT TAKES

When you believe in the inevitably of your success, everything changes. You're willing to do what most people won't do.

Most distributors get started with an attitude of, "Let's see what happens". When things don't work the way they expected, they often slow down or quit.

Some distributors have a better attitude. They say, "I'll do my best." Unfortunately, their best may not be good enough. If they don't believe in themselves, they won't put in the time and effort to develop their skills or give the business enough time to grow.

The most successful distributors, the ones who believe in themselves say, "I'll do whatever it takes. No matter how hard it is or how long it takes, I'm going all the way to the top."

And they do. Because they believe they can and they're willing to do whatever it takes to do it.

In Seth Godin's book, *The Dip*, he says that in everything we do that takes sustained effort there is a "dip"—a point where most people quit. If you push through the dip, you'll achieve results most people never achieve, because you kept going, and they didn't. Godin says, "If you can get through the Dip, if you can keep going when the system is expecting you to stop, you will achieve extraordinary results."

The U.S. Navy Seals discovered that most people quit when they reach approximately 40% of their capacity. I don't know where the Dip will occur for you but when you feel like quitting, don't trust that feeling. You haven't come anywhere near your potential.

Keep going. Commit to doing whatever it takes. You won't literally have to do whatever it takes but your willingness to do it is how you will accomplish what most people don't.

THE TIPPING POINT

In network marketing there is an inverse relationship between effort and results. In the beginning, you put in much more time and effort relative to the income you earn. Later, when your organization is big enough, you reach a tipping point and your business will grow at an accelerated pace.

When the tipping point occurs, your income will quickly increase and will be disproportionate to the amount work you're doing. You earn a lot of money without putting in a lot of time.

For most of us, the tipping point doesn't occur for at least a few years. You can earn a lot of money before that. I did. But it usually takes a few years for your team to get big enough and have enough leaders building their businesses before you have enough momentum for the business to reach the tipping point and grow at an accelerated rate.

You have to know that this is the way it works so you know what to expect and you will keep building the business until it occurs.

ENJOY THE JOURNEY

I don't know how long it will take for you to reach your goals but the best way to get there is to focus on the journey, not the goals.

Focus on the process, not the results. And enjoy your journey.

You'll hear successful distributors say things like, "If you're not having fun, you're not doing it right." They find ways to have fun and be happy on their journey. They enjoy finding and working with new people and helping them achieve their goals. They enjoy spending time with their team, building friendships, working together towards the better future that's coming. They enjoy being a part of the cause and making the world a better place.

And they enjoy making money and rewarding themselves with nice things.

When they make a mistake or something goes wrong, they laugh about it and appreciate the lesson it offers.

And no matter what, they love what they do.

When you love what you do, it doesn't seem like work. The days pass quickly, you wake up eager to get to work, and before you know it, another year has passed and you've reached another milestone. If you're doing it right, you're not just building a successful business, you're building a successful life.

My years in network marketing have been a rich and rewarding journey. I hope that one day, you will look back at your journey and say the same thing.

About the Author

David M. Ward is an attorney, business owner, marketing consultant, and author.

Ward started in network marketing to build retirement income and to escape the long hours of his law practice. "I was a victim of the self-employment trap—trading my time for dollars," he says. "The bigger my practice grew, the harder I had to work."

After twenty years, he was ready for a change. "Network marketing gave me the time freedom and financial freedom I always wanted and allowed me to do things I never had the time to do when I was practicing law."

Ward has been recognized as a six-figure income earner and top recruiter in his network marketing company. He lives in southern California.

Additional Books by the Author

Recruiting Up: How I Recruited Hundreds of Professionals in My Network Marketing Business and How You Can, Too

"Recruiting up" means recruiting professionals, business owners, sales people, real estate agents, insurance brokers, financial planners, and other people with the talent and resources to build a successful network marketing business.

***

Recruit and Grow Rich: How to Quickly Build a Successful Network Marketing Business by Recruiting Smarter, Not Working Harder

"**Best MLM ebook of 2014**. . . a must for any beginner or advanced network marketer. *If I had to give my downline a book to learn network marketing with, this would be the book.*"

The author lays out the system he used to quickly identify interested prospects, expose them, and get them signed up--often in a single day.

***

Fix Your Network Marketing Business: Fire Up Your Team, Increase Recruiting and Sales, and Get Your Business Growing Again—Even if Nobody is Doing Anything

Are you frustrated with the growth of your network marketing business? Do you have trouble motivating your team? Is your genealogy a bunch of zeros? *Fix Your Network Marketing*

Business shows you how the author turned his business around when his team wasn't recruiting or selling.

✱✱✱

Network Marketing Made Simple: A Guide For Training New Distributors

Show new distributors the basics of network marketing—how to get their business started, how to recruit and make money, and how to get to the next level.

You can use this book to train new distributors, as a teaching guide on team calls, or as a self-study guide. If you have a new distributor, or you *are* a new distributor, this is the book for you.

✱✱✱

5-Minute Recruiting: Using Voicemail to Build Your Network Marketing Business

I've recruited hundreds of distributors and become a top money-earner in my company using voicemail as my primary recruiting tool. *5-Minute Recruiting* shows you how to create and use recorded voicemail messages to get more leads, recruit more distributors, and build your network marketing business.

See these books at http://recruitandgrowrich.com

Don't Forget

Get more recruiting tips with my FREE Recruiting Tips Newsletter. You'll also be notified when I release new books or have a special offer.

Subscribe here: http://recruitandgrowrich.com/newsletter

One Last Thing

If you found this book useful, please consider leaving a short review. Amazon uses reviews to rank books and many readers evaluate the quality of a book based solely on the feedback of others.

In other words, reviews are important!

Thank you for your help. I really appreciate it.

Also, if you would like to send me your comments about this book, or suggestions for future books, please email me at recruitingbook@gmail.com

I'd love to hear from you.

—David M. Ward

Made in the USA
Middletown, DE
21 November 2018